A Good Parcel of English Soil

Richard Mabey

PENGUIN BOOKS

PENGUIN BOOKS

Published by the Penguin Group
Penguin Books Ltd, 80 Strand, London WC2R ORL, England
Penguin Group (USA) Inc., 375 Hudson Street, New York, New York 10014, USA
Penguin Group (Canada), 90 Eglinton Avenue East, Suite 700, Toronto, Ontario,
Canada M4P 2Y3 (a division of Pearson Penguin Canada Inc.)
Penguin Ireland, 25 St Stephen's Green, Dublin 2, Ireland (a division of Penguin Books Ltd)
Penguin Group (Australia), 707 Collins Street, Melbourne, Victoria 3008, Australia
(a division of Pearson Australia Group Pty Ltd)
Penguin Books India Pvt Ltd, 11 Community Centre, Panchsheel Park, New Delhi – 110 017, India
Penguin Group (NZ), 67 Apollo Drive, Rosedale, Auckland 0632, New Zealand
(a division of Pearson New Zealand Ltd)
Penguin Books (South Africa) (Pty) Ltd, Block D, Rosebank Office Park, 181 Jan Smuts Avenue,
Parktown North, Gauteng 2193, South Africa

Penguin Books Ltd, Registered Offices: 80 Strand, London WC2R ORL, England

www.penguin.com

First published in Penguin Books 2013
001

Copyright © Richard Mabey, 2013
All rights reserved

The moral right of the author has been asserted
'On a Ruined Farm near the His Master's Voice Gramophone Factory' by George Orwell
(copyright © George Orwell, 1933) reprinted by kind permission of A.M. Heath & Co Ltd.

Set in 11.75/15pt Baskerville MT Std
Typeset by Jouve (UK), Milton Keynes
Printed in England by Clays Ltd, St Ives plc

ISBN: 978-1-846-14616-9

www.greenpenguin.co.uk

ALWAYS LEARNING   **PEARSON**

If you're trying to make sense of the landscapes that shaped you as a young person it helps to have a hot spot, some metaphorical junction which connects that old space with the world you inhabit now. I'd lived for the first half of my life in the dappled shadows of the Metropolitan Line, and went on the road as a nature writer in my thirties, and I had a hunch where one such crossover might be. Somewhere west of Watford, the old straight track had to intersect with the new London Orbital. I guessed it might be in a pylon field, with scraggy horses tethered under the flyover. Then I found the exact spot on the map. The Department of Transport, maybe trying to make a point, had laid the M25 (tape cut by Margaret Thatcher in 1986) over the Metropolitan Line (opened in 1863) plumb in the middle of Chorleywood, the frontier town between suburbs and open countryside that John Betjeman had called 'essential Metro-land'. To the west lay the expanse of Chorleywood Common, a patch of real heathland, unfenced, long-grassed, with its own ancestral cricket pitch. To the east – beginning almost exactly at the flyover – was the even vaster Cedars Estate, a 500-acre borough of smart 1930s mock-Tudor villas discreetly shrouded with evergreens, that swept all the way to Rickmansworth. If there was such a thing as a commuters' ley line, this would have been its nodal point.

I couldn't tell if one could get to this *axis mundi* by road. On the map there was a bottom layer to the palimpsest of routeways, a tangle of byroads (presumably one-time footpaths across the common) which seemed to braid

with the railway, vanish, reappear, dip under
the motorway and emerge in the Cedars.
But they were easy to follow. I drove slowly
along the road that edges the common. On one
side lay the original village, a pleasant jumble
of cottages which could have come from any
part of the pre-industrial South-East. On the
other side were ponds full of gigantic aquatic
buttercups, and groups of rangy teenagers from
the local day-schools, dawdling home through
the grass like latter-day Romantics. The lane
switchbacked over and under the Met Line,
then crept through a natural cutting directly
beneath the M25.

The junction is awesome, but weirdly quiet.
The motorway rides on gigantic concrete
pillars, fifty feet high by the road and dwindling
to six or nine by the line. I watch as a Met train
slides past, with only a few inches of headroom.
Done up in London Transport's livery of red,
white and blue, it looks like something out of
Toytown. You would need to be very fanciful
to see this site as some kind of industrial henge.

It's more like a brutalist tube station. But the real Chorleywood station (non-brutalist, and still with its handsome Victorian clock) is a mile to the west, and there are no slip roads or even the slightest conceptual links between these two transport systems. A Chorleywood Metropolitan Line halt on the M25 would need a sign on the platform saying: 'Alight here for another space–time continuum.'

In 1950, A. J. Deutsch wrote a classic science fiction story called *A Subway Named Mobius*, set in a Boston tube network that has reached an almost infinite level of spatial complexity. On 4 March, the number 86 train, including more than 400 passengers, vanishes, only to rematerialize in May with the commuters still reading their ten-week-old newspapers. A mathematician brought in to advise the tube company believes the subway has become a four-dimensional version of a Möbius strip, the mathematical device in which a length of material is given a single twist and its ends are then joined, so that it has only a single surface, leading to all kinds of mysterious space–time anomalies.

The London Orbital, it seems to me, is more Möbius than the most convoluted underground system. People have been lost on it (for hours, admittedly, not weeks), circling aimlessly to find the right exit. In its early days there were coach outings devoted to its circumnavigation. For all its convenience, it is a route to nowhere, a road which simply connects with other roads. The Metropolitan Line does at least have a destination, and a mission. It exists to take people out of a working city to live in a greener place. The irony is that in doing so it has succeeded in wiping out, or at least dramatically changing, many of the green places that it used as bait for its customers. So it's also ironic, I guess, that as a boy naturalist and then a would-be Romantic scribbler, I've been endlessly enthralled by the strange and not always pretty negotiations between human and natural life that it brought into being.

The most famous of these was Metroland, a seductive term invented by the Railway Company's publicity team to describe the area – chiefly inside the Chiltern hills' mosaic of beechwoods and commons – where it had had the nous to buy up parcels of land on which to build houses for its potential customers, thus cannily providing both the honeytrap and the beeline. Metroland was a grandiose and sometimes cynical concept designed to encapsulate the urban worker's dream of a country retreat, wreathed by wild flowers and birdsong but not too far from the office. Its inventors planned to create a suburban Arcadia for commercial profit.

It certainly became classic suburbia. Whether it was ever Arcadian, or even faux-rural, is debatable. But it has obstinately survived, and is a candidate for that fashionable new category of landscape, 'edge-land'. Victor Hugo in *Les Misérables* called this kind of undefined, hybrid habitat *terrain vague*, a landscape 'somewhat ugly but bizarre, made up of two different natures, which surrounds certain great cities'. 'To observe the city edge,' Hugo wrote, 'is to observe an amphibian. End of trees, beginning of roofs, end of grass, beginning of paving stones, end of ploughed fields, beginning of shops, the end of the beaten track, the beginning of passions, the end of the murmur of things divine, the beginning of the noise of humankind.' Except that the original vision of Metroland was not one of such sharp ends and beginnings, but one where trees, pavements, fields, moments of rhapsody and trips to the shops would be seamlessly interleaved. Such a harmonious marriage did materialize in a few places, until the noise of humankind became too overpowering. But something else also began to take shape around Metroland, a fraying of its neat edges, a wayward outgrowth that seemed to me, scavenging for ideas in it for much of my life, more interestingly mutable, and more inspiringly upstart than any part of its sedate interior.

There's a concept in ecology which may be useful here. An 'ecotone' is a zone where one habitat merges with another, creating something with a character more than the sum of its parts. A salt marsh is an ecotone. There is sea on one side and dry land on the other, but between them a hinterland that is, in a more than metaphorical sense, a world of shifting sands. The scrubby zone between a wood and open fields is an ecotone. There are mature trees and the tabula rasa of grassland, but, squabbling between them, a mobile strand of brambles and thorn. Ecotones have no real edges and are inherently unstable. The habitats on either side of them continually advance and retreat. Their inhabitants, microclimates, topographies are constantly being shuffled. Modern Metroland is too settled these days to be a pure ecotone. But it lies in the broad margin between city and open countryside, and through it and round it ecotonic muddles and relics proliferate. And ecotones are where things happen.

Down in the cutting under the M25/Met Line synapse, I can see the funereal canopy of the Cedars Estate's shrubberies directly ahead and glimpse the mock-Tudor villas they shelter. I grub about among the pillars instead, peering at the weeds. They're an unexceptional waste-ground mix: thistles, purple toadflax, tall sprays of hemlock with liver-spotted stems, busy clumps of that ancestral midden species fat hen. I climb gingerly up towards the line, wondering if debris from the passing road traffic has contributed to the delectation of passing rail passengers, peering through their sealed windows at the beginning of the green belt. Tomato bushes and holly trees have appeared in places like this, sprung from the seeds in thrown-out burgers or the berries from crash-site votive wreaths. But there are no such floral parables. Then I spot the ivy, one of Metroland's signature species, restored to rustic respectability when the young Queen Victoria began wearing diamond-studded ivy wreaths in her hair. It's snaking its erratic way up at least four of the concrete pillars and has already reached more than six feet high. On one of the columns nearest the road, I can just make out a maze of faint reticulations where an earlier generation of tendrils has been scraped off. That first invasion of ivy can't have begun much more than thirty years ago, yet these fossil traces already look like prehistoric graffiti. The ivy's story is typical of the constantly changing fortunes of nature in edge-lands. A species that is a natural climber of trees in the wild (not a parasite, incidentally; it simply uses the trunk as scaffolding) finds a man-made artefact, in this case a concrete motorway pillar twenty-five years old, and scales it exactly as it would an immemorial English oak. It even has the louring shadow of the motorway to act as a simulacrum of woodland shade. Then humans notice the impertinent intruder and eradicate it from their modernist monument. The ivy, of course, still lurks, in buried seeds and root fragments, and soon begins a new ascent. Nothing short of a scorched-earth policy (not Chorleywood's style) would exterminate it altogether.

But it occurs to me that this ivy is an emblem

not just of the opportunist liveliness that dogs the edges of Metro country, but of my own clingy attachments to it. For much of my life I've been rooted elsewhere, but seem to have repeatedly sent out compulsive suckers towards these perverse, ambivalent, occasionally downright weird but always inspiring backlands. I was born on the fringe of Metroland in the 1940s and spent my childhood running wild in its leftover patches. I came to work in another stretch in my twenties and ever since have been drawn, either literally or in my imagination, by its provocative contrariness. Looking back at the line's history as I write, I'm intrigued by the way its development, its marriage of pastoral and technological dreams, mirrors my own.

The opening of the Metropolitan Line – the world's first urban railway to burrow underground – occurred in the same year (1863) as Professor Lidenbrock's subterranean adventures in Jules Verne's fantasy *Voyage to the Centre of the Earth*, and one way of looking at

the London underground is as an expression
of nineteenth-century futurism. It grew out
of a brew of pastoral dreams, utopian social
engineering and sheer technological daredevilry.
And out of classic Victorian contradiction.
It was a railway to get you away from the
railway system.

The development of London railways in
the nineteenth century was always bound to be
a vicious circle. The more the city's businesses
expanded, the greater the number of workers
they needed and the less space there was
available for them to live in. Moving home-
space ever further away from work-space
became inevitable, and as the infrastructure of
travel itself began to occupy an increasing area
of inner-city land, the centrifugal migration
of London's population became inexorable.
The pioneering main-line termini which were
built in London in the 1830s, at London Bridge,
Euston and Paddington, were all intrusions into
poor working-class areas, where property prices
were low and the displaced population unlikely

to kick up a fuss. The clearance of entire neighbourhoods was carried out on a scale that would only be matched a century later in the Blitz. In *Dombey and Son*, Dickens describes the mayhem caused by bulldozing the London to Birmingham line through Camden:

> Houses were knocked down; streets broken through and stopped; deep pits and trenches dug in the ground; enormous heaps of earth and clay thrown up . . . There were a hundred thousand shapes and substances of incompleteness, wildly mingled out of their places, upside down, burrowing in the earth, aspiring in the air, mouldering in the water, and unintelligible as any dream . . . In short, the yet unfinished and unopened railway was in progress.

The painter John Martin, doyen of what was called 'the apocalyptic sublime', echoed this vision of what might be either the beginning or the end of the world. His epic canvas *The Last Judgement* (1853) features the moment of Revelation in full swing under a blood-red sunset. But approaching from the background is a train. Whether it is on a rescue mission or carrying the Devil isn't clear, but its presence catches the ambivalence of the first railways, simultaneously destroyers and liberators of London's warrens.

Where it wasn't bound, it hardly needs saying, was the wealthy estates of the West End. The London and Birmingham line stopped abruptly north of the Euston Road, just as the City of London Corporation had only permitted one small penetration, at Fenchurch Street. Getting between London's centre and the railway stations, for gadabouts and workers alike, meant going by hackney carriage or horse-drawn omnibus (there were more than 200,000 horses in London, some housed in multi-storey stables). By the 1840s, adding to the misery caused by slum clearance and railway construction, there was something close to gridlock on the London streets, especially in the labyrinthine lanes of the City.

Enter Charles Pearson, who was in the

powerfully incongruous position of being both a radical and Solicitor to the Corporation of London. Pearson believed in the potential social benefits of the railways, but had seen first-hand the social havoc they were causing. And he had a possible solution, which he began to advocate to the Corporation. He'd noticed that the London poor were keen on weekend outings to the countryside around London, and that the better-off were moving out to the same regions and travelling back during the week. The word commuting hadn't yet been invented, and he described these movements as 'oscillations', a term which sounds oddly mechanical now but was at least inclusive of both varieties of back-and-forth migration. Why not, Pearson reasoned, deliberately plan a railway to provide for such regular human tides, and, to avoid the socially unfair devastation caused by the main lines, build it *under the ground*?

His first plan, set out in 1839, was for a wide, covered cutting that would connect a huge, half-underground station at Farringdon with the national main-line system. It would also (and the dream of Metroland begins to emerge here) connect up with new estates for poorer city workers, which, he argued, should be built six miles to the north. But his vision was too far into the realms of science fiction ever to become a reality – 'more Fritz Lang's *Metropolis*', Andrew Martin suggests, 'than metropolitan railway'. Pearson's dream train would be drawn by atmospheric power, a 'rope of air'. Trains would be attached to pistons set in a pipe between the rails, which were in their turn then sucked along by pumping engines. This idea of an ethereal source of transport energy – smokeless, whisperingly quiet, a metaphorical zephyr blowing beneath the smog-ridden streets – was faddish in the mid-nineteenth century, and echoed the contemporary fantasy of piping wholesome air from Hampstead Heath down into the Great Wen's miasmic centre. Joseph Paxton, who had designed the Crystal Palace, went so far as to publish plans for an air-powered 'Great Victorian Way', a 72-foot-wide glass arcade around the whole of central London that resembled a gigantic circular shopping mall – or perhaps a prophetic vision of the M25.

A few atmospheric-powered railways were built in remote places, but none on the scale or with the underlying sense of mission of Pearson's scheme. The outline he put to the Royal Commission on Metropolitan Termini was full of philanthropic zeal and belief in the redemptive power of the rural experience:

> The passion for a country residence is increasing to an extent that it would be impossible to persons who do not mix much with the poor to know. You cannot find a place where they do not get a broken teapot in which to stuff, as soon as spring comes, some flower or something to give them an idea of green fields and the country.

Pearson's plans ran up repeatedly against vested interests, but eventually the Metropolitan Line opened on 10 January 1863. The *Illustrated London News*'s report likened the atmosphere on opening day to a show-biz premiere, but with hindsight it reads like a vision of the rush-hours of the future:

> . . . it was calculated that more than 30,000 persons were carried over the line in the course of the day. Indeed, the desire to travel by this line on the opening day was more than the directors had provided for; and from nine o'clock in the morning till past midnight it was impossible to obtain a place in the up or City-ward line at any of the mid stations. In the evening the tide turned, and the crush at the Farringdon-street station was as great as at the doors of a theatre on the first night of some popular performer.

When it got down to serious business the Metropolitan Railway company agreed to Pearson's pressure for cheap workmen's fares on the Met (something that was later made a legal condition for the company extending its lines). In an 1865 pamphlet, Henry Mayhew, the great champion of the London poor, interviewed workmen who were making use of the line and its cheap fares. His vivid description of an early morning at Paddington hints at how close the countryside – and a recognizably rural 'style' – was to the centre of London. The platform was 'a bustle with men, a large number of whom had bass [i.e. wicker] baskets in their hands, or tin flagons, or basins done up in red handkerchiefs. Some few carried large saws under their arms.' One of his interviewees explained that he lived in Notting Hill – then 'almost in open country' – and that he was able to afford two rooms for what one cost in the centre of London. The Metropolitan Line was beginning to drive the border between town and country further west from its very inception, decades before the invention of Metroland.

Charles Pearson died the year before the Metropolitan Line officially opened, and ten years later the board appointed a very different kind of man to become its chairman. Sir Edward Watkin was a hard-headed northern businessman, with railway interests all over England, including the Manchester, Sheffield and Lincolnshire Railway, the South Eastern and the French Chemin de Fer du Nord. And he had a private agenda for the Met. He wanted it to be the London section of a mega-railway joining Paris (where he reputedly kept a mistress) with his home town, Manchester (where he kept a wife). It would have involved a considerably more daring adventure in the bowels of the earth than any of the London tube diggings, and in the delicious understatement of one of his aides, he was 'frustrated only by the political and financial problems bound up with constructing a channel tunnel'.

Watkin did create his trunk line in the end, and the Great Western Railway opened in 1897. He died in 1901, and didn't see the full flowering of his personal cut-and-cover run. But in the preceding years he had been driving the Metropolitan Line 'extension' ever further westwards. The potential problems of suffocation posed by having steam trains in enclosed tunnels had been solved by the

development of 'condensing' devices, in
which the exhaust fumes were passed through
cold-water tanks on board the locomotive.
So the line pushed on, reaching Swiss Cottage
in 1868, Harrow, Pinner and Neasden in the
1880s, Rickmansworth in 1887, Chesham
in 1889, Aylesbury in 1892 and Uxbridge, on a
branch line, in 1904. On the way some station
jewels were created that have since vanished.
St John's Wood is now on the Jubilee Line, but
was originally a Met halt, just half a mile from
Lord's Cricket Ground. For a few months in the
summer of 1939, at the urging of the MCC, it
was renamed Lord's Station, until it was closed
in November of that year. Its remains now lie
under the Danubius Hotel, Regent's Park.

Meanwhile the Metropolitan Railway was
prudently buying up parcels of pleasantly rural
land around the line far in excess of what was
needed for the permanent way itself – and in
the process exposing (for anyone who didn't
already know) what vast swathes of England
were owned by Oxbridge colleges and the

Church. In 1908 Robert Hope Selbie became general manager of the Metropolitan and saw that there were other, more feasible business opportunities than using the Met as part of a link between Paris and the North-West. The company was perfectly positioned not just physically to transport workers between the city and the country, but to sell them an entire rural dream. It would build rose-wreathed cottages that would tempt commuters to live outside London and therefore be in need of the company's trains to get home: the market as Möbius strip. Over the next few years Selbie engineered a number of private Acts and legal loopholes that gave the Metropolitan Railway the right to do what had previously been forbidden by its constitution: to buy and develop land for purposes other than railway use, without any statutory sanction or time limit (chiefly by hiving such activities on to a separate but associated company). A few years later, the chairman of the Metropolitan Railway, Sir Clarendon Golding Hyde, had the brass to put a public-service gloss on the building bonanza that ensued: 'The Metropolitan has always had one definite policy. It was that whenever the jaded Londoner went northwards in pursuit of his ideals – open air and a garden – there the Metropolitan tried to follow him.' But from the outset it was clear that the Metropolitan was in the van, dangling a home-grown carrot.

Just how the term 'Metroland' (or 'Metro-land', as the company preferred to spell it) originated is the subject of various urban legends. One version attributes it to James Garland, a copywriter employed by the company's Advertising and Publicity department. Another traces it to a verse by the journalist George Robert Sims which succinctly, if wincingly, sets the tone of the image-building that was to follow:

I know a land where the wild flowers grow,
Near, near at hand if by train you go,
Metro-land, Metro-land.
Meadows sweet have a golden glow.
Hills are green in the Vales below . . .

Leafy dell and woodland fair,
Land of love and hope and peace,
Land where all your troubles cease,
Metro-land, Metro-land,
Waft, O waft me there.

Whatever its origins, it was an inspired naming, evoking a fairy-tale Avalon that could be reached by the modern magic carpet of an electrified railway. That year it became the title of the company's annual guide, and the prompt for a whole new design. The cover of the 1915 edition ('Price One Penny') carried a full-colour painting of a bright young thing, in bonnet and long white dress, picking flowers in a tree-fringed meadow; and subsequent issues all featured rustic images of Chiltern landscapes or classic Metroland mock-Tudor houses. The contents praised the amenities of various areas along the line, and included announcements of properties for sale on the new mushrooming estates.

In the early editions, the appeal of the Met

Line's province to weekend pleasure-seekers (including fossil hunters and clay-pigeon shooters) was strongly underlined, as for instance in the copy about the Orchard Bungalow and Field at Ruislip, 'An Ideal Resort . . . for School Outings, Bands of Hope and Other Parties', and there were advertisements for maps and rambling guides. Golf especially was offered up as the *sport du pays*. There were at least eighteen golf courses being advertised in Metro-land by 1920, not just as destinations for a day's play, but as pleasant and convenient amenities to have at the end of the garden. The stress on the physical, and often it seemed spiritual, health to be found at the end of the line was endorsed by Selbie himself, who wrote in *The Railway Yearbook* for 1930 that 'Metro-land lays definite claim to be the most healthy district round London.'

The great campaign worked. Over the next ten years property developers unrolled Metroland estates all the way from Wembley Park to

Chesham. The grandest was the Cedars
Estate, built on 500 acres of farmland between
Chorleywood and Rickmansworth, which the
estate-management arm of the Metropolitan
Railway bought for £24,000 in 1919.

The houses sold as soon as they were on
the market, as the fairy tale of Metroland was
playing to a receptive (one is tempted to say
captive) audience. It had been launched during
the tail end of a widespread reaction against
the industrialization and urbanization of the
countryside, a feeling that had found expression
in phenomena as diverse as the Arts and Crafts
movement, the 'flight to the land' and the
pastoral poetry of the Georgians. It reached its
fullest flowering in the aftermath of the Great
War, when there was a popular yearning for the
green fields of old England as an antidote to the
obscene horrors of the trenches, and a fit place
for homes and gardens for the returning soldiers.
In 1926 the Prime Minister, Stanley Baldwin,
published a eulogy for rural England that could
have come straight from a Metroland brochure:

The wild anemones in the woods in April, the last load of hay being drawn down a lane as twilight comes on, when you can scarcely distinguish the figures of the horses as they take it home to the farm, and above all, most subtle, most penetrating and most moving, the smell of wood smoke coming up in the autumn evening, or the smell of the scotch firs; that wood smoke that our ancestors, tens of thousands of years ago, must have caught on the air when they were coming home from a day's forage.

An appeal to such sentiments was a powerful part of the government's programme for national unity in the troubled 1920s.

But there is an intriguing feudal footnote to this story of the mostly democratic colonization of the Chilterns. The Met's commuter traffic pretty much petered out at Aylesbury. But during the 1890s the company extended their line deep into rural Bucks and Oxfordshire, through Waddesdon, Quainton Road, Brill

and Grandborough Road, ending at Verney
Junction. This was largely because of pressure
from the Duke of Buckingham at Wotton
and his neighbour Sir Harry Verney (from
Claydon House), who were both on the board
of the Aylesbury and Buckingham Railway.
The ABR ran six miles of track from Aylesbury
to Quainton Road, and connected up with
the 'Brill Tramway', the Duke's private line to
his estate. In 1891 Sir Edward Watkin saw the
potentialities of this stretch of line as another
jigsaw piece in his grand dream of a super-
railway (perhaps it should have been called the
Cosmopolitan) between Paris and Manchester,
and persuaded the Met to buy out the ABR.

The Quainton Road/Verney Junction
extension now became an extraordinary
hybrid, though well within the limits of Met
Line eccentricity. It transported London horse
manure out for the Duke of Buckingham's
farms at night and ferried the local toffs to
and from the City during the day – in some
style. It had two Pullman carriages (named

Mayflower and Galatea) with window blinds of green silk, and above each seat, marvelled the *Railway Magazine* in 1910, was 'an ormolu luggage rack with finely chased ornamentation and panels of grass treillage', while glass-topped tables were lit by 'a tiny portable electrolier of a very chaste design'. Whisky was served en route in crystal glasses.

In the end, this forelock-tugging by the Met had to give way to commercial hard-headedness. The number of travellers out as far as Verney Junction was often in single figures, and starting in 1932 with Waddeson, these outer-limit halts were closed. Brill went in 1935 and Verney Junction in 1936, though the latter remained open for goods traffic until 1947.

With the onset of economic depression in the 1930s, the development of Metroland slowed down, and with it the fortunes of the company. The government drew up plans to take overall control of London's passenger transport, and in June 1933 the Metropolitan Railway Company ceased to exist and was absorbed into what was soon called simply London Transport. The Second World War brought all housing development abruptly to a halt, and the raft of Town and Country Planning Acts in the 1950s and 1960s severely controlled it in rural areas such as the Chilterns. Now, in 2013, it's a different, privatized world. New upmarket estates are popping up sporadically right across Metroland's old territories, and new entrepreneurial railway companies are joining up lines in a way that must have Sir Edward Watkin cheering in his grave. But the spirit of Metroland – a territory in the mind as much as on the ground, neighbourly, sentimental, oddball, accommodating and forever fraying at the edges, continues to thrive.

The story of how the Mabeys arrived on the fringes of Metroland three years after the Metropolitan Railway disappeared has become a modest legend in our family. I think we were simply chuffed to have found a moment of real prescience in our dad's life, which had later petered out in illness and disappointment. But looking back at the story now, its ingredients seem to echo those of the Metroland myth itself: the shining hope of technology, the escape from turmoil, the green haven at the end of the line.

I remember hearing the full (and doubtless slightly embellished version) just after my dad died in the 1960s, when I was just twenty. We were sitting in what was virtually a Metroland theatre – the 'lounge' of our detached 1930s house on the edge of Berkhamsted, with its view through the 'French windows', over rows of box and laurel hedges, to a strip of undeveloped parkland and the cedars of Lebanon from which our road got its name. And we were riffling through an old brochure of business machines. Inside was a picture of my dad's own invention, the fully patented 'May-bee' automated ledger book. He'd worked as an accounts clerk in a City bank in the 1930s (riding the Northern Line from Norwood then) but had been spotted as having a gadgeteer's mind and an intuitive understanding of accounting machines. In the mid-1930s he was sent to Germany as part of a contingent to scout out new business technology. They'd toured the big machine companies, and their hosts had boasted of German factories' flexibility, and of how easily they could be converted into, say, small-arms manufacture. By a bleak but providential coincidence, the party was staying at the same hotel as a National Socialist rally at which Hitler (and Dad swore he saw him) was in attendance to give one of his psychotic performances. Dad returned home with no doubts about what was going to happen, and in 1936 moved my mother and their small daughter out of London, away from the bombs to come.

The reason they chose the Chilterns never made it into the family myth, except, perhaps, that it was the first stretch of open countryside which from a German point of view was on the far side of London. But the nagging lure of Metroland must have played a role too. My father was a curious kind of techno-patriot who could easily have escaped from an H. G. Wells novel, and the idea of a retreat in Deep England from which you could be effortlessly beamed into the commercial centre of London would have appealed to him.

What was on offer, just a score of miles north-west of the capital, was the dream of satisfying two strong and contrasting human drives: to be both settled native and adventurous pioneer. The Metropolitan company's pitches at helping their customers resolve these dreams were masterpieces of arcane double-speak, blending antiquarian nostalgia with an appeal to the frontier spirit, and subliminally suggesting a kind of resonance, a continuity, between the ancestral journeys of fieldworkers and their clients' daily forays to and from the City:

> This is a good parcel of English soil in which to build home and strike root, inhabited from old, as witness the lines of camps on the hill tops and

confused mounds amongst the woods, the great
dyke which crossed it east and west, the British
trackways, the Roman Road aslant the eastern
border, the packhorse ways worn deep into
the hillsides, the innumerable fieldpaths which
mark the labourers' daily route from hamlet
to farm. The new settlement of Metroland
proceeds apace, the new settlers thrive amain.
[*Metro-land* brochure, 1927, a year after Stanley
Baldwin's appeal.]

The spot our family had fetched up in,
the expanding Hertfordshire market town of
Berkhamsted, wasn't on the Metropolitan Line
itself (Dad commuted, usually, from the local
LMS main-line station), but it was, in character
and by definition, squarely in Metroland. The
company mapped out its signature estate as
the land which lay up to five miles either side
of the line, a penumbra (or perhaps 'curtilage',
to use an aptly antique estate agent's term) of
countryside which straggled almost 50 miles
from Baker Street to the remote heart of north

Buckinghamshire. Our nearest Met station was only four miles to the south, at Chesham, so we were passport-carrying citizens of the new Arcadia. And we had all the accoutrements that made up 'a good parcel of English soil', as laid down in the company's manifesto. Stretches of Grim's Ditch, part of the 'great dyke' system that divided up the tribal ranches of the Iron Age Chilterns, snaked through commons north and south of our house. There were mysterious mounds in most of the woods and Berkhamsted High Street itself was partly a Roman road. Even the origins and character of the new community in which our house was situated replicated those of Metroland's core in their combination of urban opportunism and do-it-yourself backwoodsmanship.

Cedar Road was part of a new housing estate built on what had once been the landscape park of Berkhamsted Hall, the residence of Graham Greene's uncle Charles. The Hall's estate, like many others, was broken up just after the First World War. The western half of its grounds was sold off for council houses in the mid-1920s, the eastern for 200 red-brick commuters' dwellings ten years later. (They were advertised as 'homesteads', adding an instant sense of old habitation.)

But this is where our neighbourhood's story starts to wander from the utopian blueprint laid down by the Metropolitan Railway. The two new settlements were separated by about 100 acres of the old park – rough grassland, specimen trees, terraced tennis courts, walled gardens, all the trappings of a grand estate – which remained as an undeveloped no-man's-land, slowly returning to the wild. It became, of course, an adventure playground for every child that lived in its two contrasting estates, which could just see each other across the park. Grammar Diggers and Council Bugs (as we called each other) glowered across the scrub like rival football supporters, jealous, respectively, of the other's street skills and home privileges. But we rubbed along, as adjacent tribes must do, and somehow worked out a code of territorial rights and acceptable behaviour. The Hall itself survived for a while as a boys' prep school, but became infested with rot and had to be demolished. Its brick remains lay like two long tumuli at the foot of the park, full of cryptic secrets and possibilities.

When I began seriously exploring this wilderness in the early 1950s (our neighbourhood gang of nine- to twelve-year-olds called it The Field, as if it were the only one in Creation), it had evolved into a kind of common, and was not being played in by the sedate rules of Metroland at all. Our dads dug up turfs from the park's derelict lawns to lay on their own modest greenswards, and recycled the Hall's elegant bricks and marble in their garden walls. They were mostly city workers, and walking to and from the station they wore out their own 'innumerable' footpaths, based around a diagonal transect across The Field, from which small side-tracks radiated to individual back-garden gates. With an entrepreneurial spirit that matched that of the railway company, our

gang recognized the market potential of this
regular throughway and its captive audience,
and set up an orange-box stall alongside it,
under one of the park's great walnut trees.
We nicked vegetables from our fathers' gardens
and sold them back to the hapless growers as
they trudged home for supper, too tired and
vulnerable (and maybe a mite proud of our
cheek) to resist. In the landscape between,
increasingly a jungle of feral ornamental trees
and burgeoning hawthorn scrub, we created our
own network of camps and inscrutable mounds,
impressive in their complexity and aboriginal
sense of occupation despite a total absence of
provenance, and acted out the fantasy of being
Amazonian explorers. We learned to cook on
wood fires, churn butter on upturned bicycles,
build huts, invent a kind of Lord of the Flies
sex, and devise ways of torturing kids from
the council estate when they strayed across
our boundaries – all entirely proper skills for
pioneering settlers.

I'm not sure quite what my concept of 'nature'

was at this age. I'd already, rather precociously, begun reading (and shamelessly plagiarizing in my school English essays) the nineteenth-century rural writer Richard Jefferies. I was especially smitten by his collection *Wild Life in a Southern County* (1879), with its rhapsodic descriptions of chalk hills and ancient trackways. I had no idea then that in the late 1870s he was already living in the Surrey suburbs and penning essays with titles like 'A London Trout' and 'Trees about Town'. In 1880 he declared his belief in 'the light of the future', and wanted a world, in the words of his biographer Edward Thomas thirty years later, in which 'the light railway [would] call at the farmyard gate' – a prophetic phrase which could have become a slogan for nascent Metroland.

But my sense of nature in The Field was nothing like the self-conscious reflections of Jefferies. 'Nature' was something we all took for granted, like an extra layer of skin. We treated the great cedars of Lebanon, layered with tiers of cobwebbed wooden debris, as condominiums, and spent whole afternoons aloft in their spacious apartments. I did my first foraging, after the 'bread-and-cheese' of young hawthorn leaves, but was quite unaware that it was anything exceptional. We nicked the odd bird's egg, but regarded the owls that nested in the ruins of the Hall's old barns as familiars. Their dusk beatings around the edge of The Field – honey-coloured wings against the lime-green poplar leaves – marked out the edges of our own tribal territory. We were living in the no-man's-land between two warring systems – Metroland and the old countryside – and I suppose it is no surprise that we turned into part refugees, part pubescent guerrillas.

Our parents scarcely behaved more sedately, and used The Field as if it were a fairground site. There were community bonfires and picnics, and mass toboggan runs on steeper slopes. On Guy Fawkes Night my dad brought along giant boxes of fireworks for the entire road's delectation. His techno-sassiness also ensured that my own games in The Field were

of an advanced kind. He was fond of cruising
the army surplus stores in the City and used
to come home with bags of hardware, a kind
of military offal, along with the real tripe
he'd picked up in Smithfield meat market.
So it was that I became the proud owner, at
a dangerously young age, of an eye surgeon's
field operating kit (brilliant for cutting balsa
wood accurately), a portable generator and
some USAF meteorological box-kites. They
flew triumphantly over the tawny grassland,
as did the rubber-powered model aircraft I'd
laboriously built from balsa frames and lacquered
tissue skins. But it was the Jetex-fuelled planes
that were the real 'light of the future'. The Jetex
engine (now classed as an explosive and illegal
to sell) was a small tube into which you plugged
a fast-burning solid-fuel cartridge. When it was
lit, using a long fuse, it produced such a thrust
that the planes sped off at astonishing speed,
often quite low, and came perilously close to the
neighbourhood greenhouses.

With hindsight it looks as if, young and old,

we were all acting out an unconscious parody of
Metroland and the pomposity of its advertising
campaign. But at the time, I felt a simple thrill
in the repeated clashes between the supposed
respectability of the place I lived and played in,
and the feral forces of young imaginations and
wild regeneration. We once set the grassland on
fire for a dare, and scattered into the bushes in
a kind of crazed excitement. We tried to ride
the Highland cattle a local smallholder put out
to graze there. We went back reluctantly to
our homes at teatime with bites and scars and
stories we would never dare tell our parents. We
were all Metro-kids, with no rural backgrounds,
and I've no idea of the origins of our intuitive
understanding of The Field, of which leaves
made the best camp roofing and which woods
the best fires. But those days imprinted me with
a sense that the border between the domestic
world and the wild was porous and mobile; that
wherever there was development there would
be creative disintegration; and that alongside
all straight, organizing staves like railway lines,

some life would always move in an improvised, syncopated rhythm, *contrametro*.

I began drifting towards the Met's heartland as soon as I could ride a bike, aged about eleven, I guess. Metroland was created on the assumption of an instinctive itch to migrate west, following the movement of the sun, to where, as Thoreau believed, the land was 'more unexhausted and richer'. But we lived north of the line, and my natural compass seemed from the beginning to have been set southwards. South was where the hills began, where the winter bournes rose like rippling silver eels, where even the wayside cow parsley seemed frothier.

The Met Line and I were both arrowing in, from different directions, on the Chiltern heartlands, a region too abstract to make any topographical sense to me at that age, but which held me in a powerful spell. There was a point on a hilltop where I would always pause on my cycle ride to school cricket, and gaze in something close to rapture at the scene that unfolded southwards, the rising hills, the ancient beech groves, the ashwood where the first chiffchaff always sang . . . 'It was an unsettling feeling,' I wrote later, 'numinous, indefinable, a sense of something just beyond reach. At times it turned into an actual physical sensation that made the back of my legs tighten, as if I were peering down from a great height.' All the runes pointed towards Chesham, where, quite unbeknown to me at the time, the Metropolitan Line came to a ceremonious full stop against a set of buffers. I was more impressed by the way the locals pronounced the town's name (Chez-ham, after the River Chess, which flowed through it, not Chesh-am) than by the fact that it was a major local freight station, famous for ferrying the town's three B's – boots, beer and brushes – to the London markets.

By the time I had a car I was using the countryside just north of the line between the stations at Chesham and Chalfont & Latimer as an alfresco *pied à terre*. Whenever things in Berkoland seemed too stale or reserved

(The Field, with a terrible irony, was swallowed up by a Metroland-style estate in the 1960s), I'd take off to this luxuriant patch alongside the Chess, where the bluebells bloomed earlier and swallows arrived sooner. I went south, I think, quite deliberately to meet spring on its way north.

I was a walker in the William Hazlitt mould in those days, using regular routes as a source of reassurance, touching trees for luck, religiously dogging my own footsteps. 'I can saunter for hours,' Hazlitt wrote, 'bending my eye forward, stopping and turning to look back, thinking to strike off into some less trodden path, yet hesitating to quit the one I am on, afraid to snap the brittle threads of memory.' I settled into a ritual clockwise walk, increasingly threaded with memories, through the water meadows on the north side of the river, then back along the foot of a beechwood and a network of green lanes. It was the kind of journey you could make in almost any chalk-country valley, but the Metropolitan Line was only a mile to the south, and even at that distance it changed things. The aura of suburbia it generated seeped through the surrounding countryside, but nature argued back, *contrametro*, and these buffer-lands alongside the line were rowdy with dissonance. Things appeared here which were unthinkable eight miles further north, like the six calling cuckoos I once saw together in a single meadow. The river helped. The Chess was a real chalk stream, and it eddied through a complex series of creeks and S-bends here, so that straightforward ecological muddle was added to the mistier questions of landscape identity.

The basic unit of field division in this patch of the Chilterns, heavily settled as it was by the aspirant middle classes, was the weekend and after-school-hours paddock for young girls' ponies. But there were no neat post-and-rail fences yet, and hedges that dated back to before the Norman invasion crowded into rough water meadows full of improvised oil-barrel jumps. Watercress beds (the crop was taken on piled-high lorries to the Met Line freight depot at Chesham) edged into the lower parts of the woods. So did kingfishers, which occasionally shot like meteors between the lower branches. The woods retaliated, and after storms, beech trunks lay slowly mouldering in the water and irritating the fly-fishers. I loved one familiar of these fallen trees in particular, the bracket fungus known as beech tuft. The glutinous white caps were partly translucent and became slightly droopy as they aged, so that they often took on the form of the melting watch in Salvador Dalí's painting *The Persistence of Memory*. To which faculty they greatly contributed: sprouting limply from trunks almost submerged in the water, they had the look of ectoplasmic lotus blossom.

The woodland flowers were special too, especially in Mounts Wood. This was a thin fillet of beechwood, sandwiched between the river and the slope south to Chorleywood, but it had an extraordinary collection of ancient woodland specialities: sweet woodruff, yellow

archangel, wood anemone – even their names
sounded like a forest carol. Best of all, it
contained what is virtually the signature plant
of Metroland, coralroot, which grows nowhere
in Britain save the gravelly woods between
Watford and Chesham and a few patches in the
Kentish Weald. It's a plant of extraordinary
grace, like a woodland lady's-smock, with larger,
darker pink flowers and with purple-brown
bulbils at the base of the leaves. In those days
in my early thirties I was in thrall to an elfin
ecologist who happened to live at the London
end of the Metropolitan Line. One afternoon
in early May, in an attempt to woo her to either
my charms or those of my Metro homeland
(I'm truly not sure which), I tracked down a
patch of Mounts Wood's very best, my shot at
laying out a suburban version of Titania's floral
couch in *A Midsummer Night's Dream*. When we
stopped to peer down at it, the effect of the
maze of filigree plants – the whorls of viridian
woodruff leaves, the coralroot's pale rubies,
the waving wands of wood melick grass, all set

against tuffets of moss – was so overpowering, such a miniature cameo of the wonderful variety of life, that I quite lost the plot and retreated into my own private epiphany. Nature can be a very fierce romantic rival.

Even the geology has a hybrid accent here. A very distinctive local rock, which sometimes turns up in fields during deep-ploughing, is puddingstone. It's a conglomerate of all kinds of pebbles and sands, packed together by glacial drift; a natural concrete. When big specimens are found they're hauled off to adorn village greens and pub gardens, but are sometimes hijacked from one village to another. I once overheard some ramblers (mistaking what they were seeing) gravely discussing the glacial origins of a leftover pile of Second World War concrete tank traps.

This perspective, festive but also slightly dislocated, seemed to infect the other saunterers I encountered on my rounds, many of whom had come straight off the Met Line. One regular plodded the flat riverside footpaths in serious climbing boots, carrying a small dog in his arms. Two others I never saw, but I found their champagne glasses, perfectly polished, hidden in the cruck of an ancient oak, ten feet above the ground. I once crossed paths with a party of sixth-formers from a Jewish school in north London who wanted to make sure of getting back to Chorleywood station without missing any of the scenery. Could I point them on a suitable route? I did my best, and half an hour later I spotted them again, marching east well on schedule, their Hebrew songs ringing through the beechwoods.

I became familiar with another stretch of Metroland in my twenties, at the end of the branch line that runs from Harrow to Uxbridge. In the late 1960s and early 1970s, I worked in this patch, among the jumble of scrapyards and derelict canals that was scattered over much of this corner of Middlesex. I'd got a hot editorial job, at an outpost of Penguin Books, and I felt as elated as if I'd been beamed from my beechwood homeland direct to the pulsing, bohemian heart of Bloomsbury. The nature I'd worshipped as a romantic teenager went temporarily into cold storage at the back of my mind. There were, in the political and intellectual ferment of the time, other priorities.

But nature seemed disinclined to play along with the backstage role I'd given it. I could, at a pinch, have commuted from home via the LMS to Harrow and then the Met Line south. But there was an easy coach connection between Watford and the office, and it took me along a route that was the short western side of a triangle formed by the two forks of the Met, and which ran alongside a long string of active gravel diggings in the River Colne. On my hour-long journey I felt as if I were watching an eco road movie through the windows. I had glimpses of fugitive water and resplendent wildfowl glinting behind thickets of wayside scrub. The road was being constantly repaired (the M25 would soon run almost parallel with it) and on carriageways and in pits along the way immense earth-movers scrunched like glaciers through prehistoric beds of flint and gravel. On a new roundabout near Uxbridge they'd piled up an artificial sandbank, and during that first summer a colony of sand martins raised their families in the shifting bank, darting nonchalantly between the JCBs and the traffic. It was that opportunist edge-land effect again, the road builders' summer-season rubble standing in for the ancient cliff face.

It was an even more fantastical scene at work. Our outpost of the Penguin empire was shaped like a slice of cake, and wedged between a canal and a main road. When I looked through one window of my office, I gazed down on a flotsam-strewn channel edged by plants I'd never seen in my life before, from all quarters of the globe: Indian balsam, Japanese knotweed, Canadian fleabane. From the other window I could watch kestrels hovering above the rush-hour traffic on the canal bridge. I tried to imagine the Escher-like complexity of the images on their retinas: towpath jungle, pub garden, concrete and metal stream, all in different focal planes.

I used to go out exploring in my lunch hours, and found this rowdy, cosmopolitan luxuriance played out at a landscape scale, with scant respect for the Metropolitan Railway's blandishments. In July 1914 its regular leaflet series *The Met* carried an article about the region entitled 'Unknown Rural Haunts Close to London'. The reader was invited to

TAKE A TRIP to . . . Ickenham or Uxbridge. In atmosphere, though not in distance, these charming rural hamlets are hundreds of miles away.

GO WHILE NATURE IS FRESH, the birds carolling, the flowers in bloom.

HOW MANY City men know that they can be carried by THE MET straight from their offices into rural solitude where they may wander through the fields by lake and thicket in the quiet summer evening, cooled and invigorated by health-giving breezes laden with the fragrance of foliage and flowers?

The lakes and thickets just south of Uxbridge resembled this scene re-imagined by Hieronymus Bosch. My own rambles (invigorating, I concede, but far from health-giving) took me across derelict Victorian rubbish tips and through burgeoning woods of rampant Asian and Mediterranean shrubs – buddleia, bladder senna, Russian vine. I saw terns wafting over pits where the dredgers were still pulling up buckets of gravel, and great-crested grebes nesting on floating car tyres. The fragrances on the breeze were household garbage and engine oil, and the top predator was the scrapyard Alsatian guard dog. On one of my very first forays I stumbled into a plant I scarcely knew existed in Britain, a thorn apple, an aggressively bushy member of the nightshade family from the New World, with deceptively beautiful, swan-necked flowers that later develop into spiny fruits the size of conkers. These contain potent, psychotropic alkaloids, and up to a few centuries ago the seeds were used as an

anaesthetic during surgery. Wild dope – sprung
maybe from seeds in an imported Peruvian
house plant – was growing on a refuse tip just
three miles from Uxbridge tube station.

I was, for a while, emotionally lost in these
ecologically potent badlands. I felt exhilarated,
bewildered, mischievous. Despite the way
my imagination had been freed up by those
childhood days in The Field, I still shared the
conventional, anthropomorphic assumption
that industrial dereliction was as inimical to
nature as to humans. But here the wild seemed
to have a different agenda, an insistence on a
postmodern coexistence with the city, even a
hint of triumphalism. In the mood of the times,
it seemed almost insurrectionary.

It wasn't that I needed relief from the indoor
publishing routine. The work we were doing
at Penguin Education, reinventing the school
textbook, was radical and powerfully exciting.
Walking out into the bolshie exuberance of
Metroland's jungle edges seemed, in the fervid

atmosphere of the late 1960s, to be just taking the office outdoors.

This was all a long time ago. These days much of the land is being reined back into a more recognizable Metroland profile. The canal towpaths are gravelled over, and marinas for weekend narrowboats are being scalloped out along their edges. Part of the area is now inside the Colne Valley Regional Park, with its own signposted walks and interpretation boards. But many of the refuse-tip scrublands are still there, now evolving into a bizarre high forest of thirty-foot-tall buddleia, sycamore, willow and pioneering oaks. And down in the Colne's tributaries, great green wands of club-rush are swallowing the dumped fridges and lager cans.

But in trying to piece this story together, to understand better how these improbable wastes had captured my heart, and those of so many others, there were bits of Metroland I needed to experience again, and crucial stretches I'd never seen at all. One in particular lay deep in

my old Penguin *terroir*. I first saw it, tipped off
by a friend, in 2005. In the midst of a cluster
of old totters' paddocks, wedged between two
streams and close to the anglers' pub where we
often took our lunch breaks, was a rectangle
of tussocky grassland with my name on it.
'Mabey's Meadow' the London Wildlife Trust
noticeboard announced, as if I'd been martyred
there in some crucial ecological battle. (What
a shame they didn't know my father's *nom
d'invention*. 'May-bee's Meadow' would have
been much more waspishly appropriate.) I felt
slightly posthumous, and it took me a while to
find out what this flattering dedication meant.
Apparently, when the Trust took over the care
of the meadow and were casting about for a
name, they remembered that I'd helped their
ecologists survey this site back in the 1970s.
We'd found some prodigious plants there,
scarce sedges specific to ancient marshland and
the seriously odd adder's tongue, a diminutive
fern with a single bright green leaf from which
protrudes a spore-bearing blade that, to tell

the truth, is more like a green dog's cock than a snake's tongue. There was an even chance that it had been clinging on in this field for more than four centuries, the kind of ancient provenance beloved of Metroland rhapsodies. The great Elizabethan botanist John Gerard mentions it in his *Herball* of 1597, growing in meadows by this very river, the 'Col[n]e-brook'.

Going back now, on a midsummer afternoon, I can't find any trace of the fern. My meadow looks dried out and overgrazed. But true to Metro-edge form, it's ablaze with interlopers and chancers, even in 2012's notoriously appalling summer. Somehow a garden variety of Veronica has become the dominant plant, and the whole meadow is lit up by its brilliant blue spikes. It's keeping company with a host of other garden escapees – Jacob's ladder and the gaudy pink everlasting pea, both from the Mediterranean, and two species of American golden rod about to flower – and a fair scatter of native species too. The whole site looks like a floral carnival float and is dancing with butterflies.

I'm thinking that if I'm going to revisit nostalgic old haunts along the Met, maybe I ought to go by train, finally take that commute to and from Baker Street that I've never had a real reason to experience. But (my slight tube phobia rising inside me) I reject the idea. The Metropolitan Line was never intended to indulge the joy of travelling. Even though it lies mostly overground, it has always been a mole run, a corridor for getting places, not a viewing platform for what lay by the route. *Man is Born Free, and is Everywhere in Trains* runs the subtitle of Tiresias's quirky railway traveller's journal *Notes from Overground*. ('Commuter. Commuter. Commuter. Say it over and over again . . . Strange verbal resemblance to another automaton, the computer.') I decide to follow the edges instead, as I've always done, north and then west, from Uxbridge via Wembley to Amersham, the modern end of the line.

So on a cold and windy July day I drive north-east to Neasden, the scene of my next entanglement with Metroland. In 1973 I wrote

a book about my rummagings in the Middlesex
badlands called *The Unofficial Countryside*, which
the following year became the basis for a BBC
television film of the same name. We worked a
lot around the railway tracks here, filming feral
foxes and line-side flora. We got permission
to go on to the embankments and discovered
some bizarre horticultural relics. During the
war, in the 'Dig for Victory' campaign, many
householders whose gardens backed on to
the railway extended their plots on to the
embankment, which became, in effect, a linear
allotment. When the war ended, and the idea of
line-side safety overcame wartime necessity, the
beds were mostly abandoned. But the fruit and
veg lived on. Nervously exploring the Neasden
and Brent embankments (no high-visibility
jackets then), I found plots with sprawling
loganberry bushes, forests of perpetual spinach
and one vast and still-sprouting asparagus
crown over a yard wide, good parcels of English
soil migrating the other way, back into the city.

A few months later I got mud-bound in

the Welsh Harp, the big Brent reservoir that is only six miles west of Baker Street station. The reservoir had been temporarily drained and I'd walked out over the seemingly sun-baked floor with a journalist who was writing a piece about the film. We chatted about wetland plants, spotted a few migrant wading birds (and should have taken notice that they were submerged up to their knees) and then realized that we were slowly sinking. I've been half stuck in Norfolk mudflats many times, but never had the terrifying sensation of not being able to lift my feet at all. And worse, of realizing that in trying to, we were making ourselves sink even deeper. I truly believe that we might have become London's first quicksand fatalities if we hadn't spotted a gang of kids nearer the bank, having fun with the mud, but sensibly equipped with long wooden planks. We yelled to them and tried to stay very still. They were no more than ten or eleven years old, but they came out to us like a professional rescue team, laying the planks down one after the other as they edged towards us, urging us to lie flat if we could, until we were able to slither our bodies and then our mud-caked city shoes on to the blessedly supportive wood. I got to Wembley Park station reeking of decaying weed and as claggy as a frog, and hid at the back of a carriage until I got to Watford, and the less embarrassingly crowded coaches of the main-line home. It was, as I had always believed, a jungle out there on the fringes of Metroland.

But at Neasden it was impossible to ignore the presence of another shadowy traveller, shifting through the edge-lands as I was. I'd only known John Betjeman through his verses when I first made the acquaintance of Metroland. But later I discovered that the Poet Laureate of suburbia had made an exquisite, elegiac and, under Edward Mirzoeff's inspired direction, eccentrically funny film called *Metro-land* in 1973, and in it Neasden is one of the portals: 'Home of the gnome and the average citizen/ Sketchley and Unigate, Dolcis and Walpamur'

(Betjeman wrote much of his commentary in blank verse).

The film in fact begins at Baker Street station, with Betjeman sitting in the smart dining rooms of Chiltern Court. This was an upmarket development finally completed just after the First World War, with luxury flats and a restaurant where 250 people could dine as an orchestra played from the balcony, and whose name linked the urbanity of the capital with the green hills to which the Met Line would post-prandially transport them. Betjeman's accompanying words perfectly capture his ambivalence (and mine) about Metroland – the fondness for the security of the just-past, the love of ritual and the loathing of regimentation (and who cares about the inconsistency of this?): 'Here the wives from Pinner and Ruislip, after a day's shopping at Liberty's or Whiteley's, would sit waiting for their husbands to come up from Cheapside and Mincing Lane. While they waited, they could listen to the strains of the band playing for the *thé dansant* before the train took them home.'

I tracked back to new Northwood, the archetype of Metroland planning, to get a sense of how comprehensively it had changed the landscape. This was mostly open country in the early twentieth century. Now it was so entangled with a dense grid of houses that even my satnav couldn't make sense of it. But somewhere, on the road to Pinner, I passed under a Met Line bridge curved like a rainbow and painted a gorgeous Provençal blue. I watched one of the Union-flag-coloured trains slide over it, its blue stripes a more sombre shade than that of the bridge. Northwood was where the writer Julian Barnes lived in the 1950s, doing the hour-long commute to City of London School (near Blackfriars, change at Liverpool Street for the Circle Line). His first novel, *Metroland*, is a wryly funny and evocative account of what it felt like to be a self-styled existentialist teenager living in this suburban motherlode. (To *épater la bourgeoisie* was his favourite sport.) He also gives an exact description of how the 1960s trains still echoed, in their ornamentation, the fixtures and fittings of the rural dreamland they were bound for:

The carriages were high and square, with broad wooden running boards; the compartments were luxuriously wide by modern standards, and the breadth of the seats made one marvel at Edwardian femural development. The backs of the seats were raked at an angle which implied that in the old days the trains had stopped for longer at the stations . . . Above the seats were sepia photographs of the line's beauty spots – Sandy Lodge Golf Course, Pinner Hill, Moor Park, Chorleywood. Most of the original fittings remained: wide, loosely strung luggage racks with coat-hooks curving down from their support struts; broad leather window straps, and broad leather straps to stop the doors swinging all the way back to their hinges; a chunky, gilded figure on the door, 1 or 3; a brass fingerplate backing the brass door handle; and, engraved on the plate, in a tone of either command or seductive invitation, the slogan 'Live in Metroland'.

All that was missing from this mobile manorial drawing room was an on-board butler.

In doing my homework, I'd read about Eastcote station, opened on the Uxbridge branch between Rayners Lane and Ruislip in 1912. It was scarcely more than a halt to start with, the kind of place where a few milk churns might have been thrown off the train. There was no road access, only a rough footpath on the north side leading back to Ruislip station. A photograph taken more than six years later shows wooden platforms still lit by paraffin lamps and not a house in sight. But they were soon to arrive. Eastcote was destined to be the site of Metroland's equivalent of a 'model village'. A major landowner in the area was King's College, Cambridge, which, in collaboration with Ruislip Council, had drawn up plans for the development of 5,750 acres of land. The plan was liberal and idealistic.

It set out building design requirements, housing densities (12 per acre at a maximum), the location of shopping and industrial areas, even the permitted degree of outdoor advertising. For the development of the College's own 1,300-acre estate, a new company, Ruislip Manor Ltd, was formed, to create what was now looking more like a Garden City than a model village.

But then things began to proceed in a more disorderly fashion than anticipated by Ruislip's utopian planners. In the early years Eastcote Halt proved most popular not with disciples of William Morris, but with trippers from inner London. Boisterous family parties (sometimes amounting to more than 3,000 adults and kids in a day) arrived to romp in the neighbouring countryside. They especially enjoyed the delights of the Pavilion Gardens, a 16-acre site south of the railway owned and managed by a local Salvation Army bandmaster. The Metropolitan Railway Company didn't exactly help to elevate the area's image when it described Eastcote as 'a dainty little old hamlet wandering back among the centuries . . . pervaded with a farm-yard atmosphere, which the jaded town-dwellers inhales with a sigh of gratitude'. Then, in 1914, the Great War began and all building work ceased. After the war ended, there were sporadic attempts to carry the grand scheme forward, but they stuttered, and in the end most of the land was sold off to private developers.

It sounded like the possible site of another time warp. I find Eastcote station in the middle of a typical mid-twentieth-century high street – chain stores, burger bars, estate agents. Behind it is a warren of bungalows and unexceptional semis. I wander off through them, trying to get a glimpse of the line, and maybe discover the remains of that primeval footpath that carried the first commuters to the station. The network of narrow roads echoes an earlier sylvan history: Elm Avenue, Beech Avenue, Linden Avenue. Crossing them all is Oak Grove, heading in a southerly direction towards Ruislip and maybe lying over the old trackway. It crosses the Met Line by a high bridge that I can only just get my nose above. And there, soaring skywards in a cutting, is a linear forest of 100-year-old self-sown ash, oak and sycamore. The old woodiness is reasserting itself, and with typical Met-edge contrariness, doing so within acorn-drop distance of the line.

Metroland development becomes smarter the further you move away from London. As I follow the line between Pinner and Northwood, the more the roads approximate to the *rus in urbe* ideal. The houses are Metroland archetypes. They have front gardens, strips of grass on the pavement, and trim ornamental trees set at regular intervals in the grass. (There are even some old almonds, the tree of choice in our own estate in 1950s Berkhamsted, where our gang used to scrump the bitter nuts.) C. A. Wilkinson's cover illustration for the 1921 issue of *Metro-land* is a Helen Allingham-style image of a typical middle-class homestead in this zone, which would be

quite at home on a bijou tablemat. It has all
the classic ingredients of a Metroland dwelling:
gables, leaded windows, exterior timbers, steep
red tiling. There is crazy paving leading from
the front porch to a cottage-garden flower
border edged with delphiniums and polyanthus.

Betjeman's film (full, needless to say, of fits
of giggles and mute, bemused glances back at
the camera: 'What on earth am I supposed to
say about *this*?') didn't shrink from the 1970s
variations on these themes of comfortable
occupation. One sequence shows the good
people of Pinner on a Sunday, the men mowing
their lawns, the women out in the avenues
cleaning cars, while the Osmonds' track 'Down
the Lazy River' blares from transistor radios
perched on the bonnets.

But the section of line between Pinner,
Northwood and Rickmansworth marks a
crucial frontier in Metroland. Just half a mile
to the west is a large patch of real countryside,
full of ancient woods and narrow lanes, that
stretches all the way to the River Colne and the

M25. I remember exploring this in the 1970s, especially the mysterious Mad Bess Wood. According to a hoary local legend, the wood owes its name to the wife of an eighteenth-century gamekeeper, a demented old woman who prowled the woods at night looking for poachers. This is where the line passes from Middlesex into Hertfordshire, where the chalk hills of the Chilterns really begin, and where Metroland's most infamous lyricist, known simply as 'F.', reached his floweriest epiphany. It is worth quoting his essay from 1923 at some length:

> What is the peculiar charm of Metro-land? It is not 'violently lovely', as Byron said of one of his early loves, but, like her, it 'steals upon the spirit like a May-day breaking'. Its charms are many and varied. Middlesex, where it still contrives to escape the fast-spreading tide of London, wears a pleasant homely face. The elms grow tall in its fields and pastures and in the broad plain that stretches below Harrow's airy

ridge towards Uxbridge . . . But for many the best of Metro-land begins where the iron road starts to climb in among the Chilterns, which are at the very heart of Metro-land – the flinty Chilterns with their tangled ridges, their stony yet fruitful fields, their noble beech woods and shy coppices, their alluring footpaths, their timbered cottages, scattered hamlets and pretty Georgian townships strung out along the high roads . . . Only a narrow tongue of 'homely, hearty, loving Hertfordshire' lies in Metro-land, but within its pale are Rickmansworth and its lovely parks, and here is the waters-meet of Chess, Gade and Colne. Rickmansworth is a delightful old town, and Chorley Wood Common flames into yellow gold when the gorse is in flower . . . Metro-land falls short in nothing which the heart of man can desire.

Heading west towards this promised landscape – and back in a sense towards my own beginnings – I remembered how earlier generations of visionaries had created their pocket New Jerusalems among the tangled ridges and stony fields. The Levellers had cells here during the English Revolution. In 1846 the Chartists created a settlement of thirty-five smallholdings at Heronsgate, a mile beyond what would become the large holdings of the Cedars Estate. Jordans, a few miles further west, began in 1910 as a Quaker-inspired village for craftspeople. These days the Met's shrines are less ideological: the Southfork-style gates to the new estate at Breakspear House; the extravagant Gothic portico to Moor Park Golf Club, which is housed in a 1732 mansion. There was a 'golf halt' (Betjeman called it 'goff') here as early as 1910, and in 1919 Lord Ebury's 2,935-acre estate straddling the line was bought by the philanthropist Viscount Leverhulme, who promptly sold it on to Moor Park Ltd, a company created specifically to develop two more golf courses and a superior residential estate to the west. In 1923 the name of the station was officially changed to Moor Park & Sandy Lodge – adding yet another golf club to the Met's destinations. Moor Park's clubhouse is still located in Lord Ebury's palatial mansion, and must be the only nineteenth hole to be decorated with eighteenth-century *trompe-l'oeil* murals.

But move just a little to the south-west and you're on top of a low hill, with a view over fields right down into the Colne valley. And just on the far side of Harefield's heart hospital there's a hamlet on a rise called providentially 'Mount Pleasant'. I've not approached the Colne from the east before, but down in the valley it's the same feisty hinterland that I knew from my earlier explorations: angling-lake security fences, bad puns on pub signs ('The Coy Carp'), a white-water canoe slalom improvised by the edge of an industrial weir.

The river runs parallel with, and feeds into, the Grand Union Canal (the same canal that, twelve miles east, flows through Berkhamsted, underlining the magnetism that exists between railway and waterway) and I walk north along the towpath between them. The very first time I followed this track had been in the late summer of 1972, when I was struggling to find a shape for the introductory chapter to *The Unofficial Countryside*. I'd left a traffic jam on the Uxbridge–Rickmansworth road on impulse, and had found myself in this unclassifiable breathing space, with a huge industrial sewage works to the west and sheep-grazed chalk hills rising up towards Moor Park to my east. There were swallows looping under the giant pipes that carried the sewage across the canal and spikes of purple loosestrife (*Lysimachia* – the deliverer from strife!) along the water's edge. I knew straight away that this was an epitome of the book's theme, and, taking a writer's liberty, conjured up George Orwell as my companion, mainly to rebuke him for being a pessimist. In fact it was a very small liberty. In 1932 Orwell began teaching at the Hawthorns boys' prep school in Hayes, about six miles south of this stretch of the canal and only three from Uxbridge station. Hayes had been the location of HMV's original factory (I learned later that, like the factories my dad had visited in Germany in the 1930s, it too had been converted to munitions manufacture, in this case in the First World War) and Orwell had been sufficiently moved by the conjunction of industry and blighted countryside to write a poem called 'On a Ruined Farm near the His Master's Voice Gramophone Factory'.

The acid smoke has soured the fields,
And browned the few and windworn flowers;
But there, where steel and concrete soar
In dizzy, geometric towers –

There, where the tapering cranes sweep round,
And great wheels turn, and trains roar by
Like strong, low-headed brutes of steel –
There is my world, my home; yet why

So alien still? For I can neither
Dwell in that world, nor turn again
To scythe and spade, but only loiter
Among the trees the smoke has slain.

Five years later, in his novel *Coming Up for Air*, Orwell would explicitly denounce the

Metropolitan Line for its destruction of the countryside. But this was a more ambivalent, rueful elegy, acknowledging the irrevocable changes that industrialization had bought not just in the landscape, but in his outlook. A Metropolitan consciousness, once acquired, can't be magically wiped clean and the watcher restored to pastoral innocence. And I think I would have sympathized with the poem's feelings, if I hadn't spent the two previous years witnessing roaring trains and windworn trees cohabiting rather amicably in Metroland's edges.

In the 1970s there was plenty of soaring concrete. But air pollution was already declining and the trees and feral vegetation were luxuriant. Forty years on, I'm astonished by how little the place has changed. 'Yellow water lilies drooping like balls of molten wax', I'd written in 1973, and so they still were, in crystal-clear water. Naturalized buddleia, from China, is growing next to impeccably native iris. A grey wagtail loops across the cut towards the weir in the exact same place it had four decades ago. What is different is the influx of people, especially boat people. The gentrification of Chorleywood has seeped south, picking up a few bohemian and dissident shades on the way. An old bargeman's cottage with a glass-walled Bauhaus-style extension sits not a hundred yards from the narrowboat *Pisces*, emblazoned with the slogan 'Affordable boating for the community'. A pair of cormorants perform synchronized underwater dives in front of a lawn decked out with a geodesic climbing frame. There are fisherman's day-boats, floating weekend hideaways, houseboats done up in hippie baroque. Iain Sinclair, tramping the canal a mile or so further north in his circumnavigation of the M25, *London Orbital*, spotted a boat with the strapline 'Viscount Sasha, International Physiotherapist to the President of the USA'. The most eccentric I come across has a map of the entire solar system tricked out in transfers on the windscreen.

As I head towards Ricky, there are blackcaps, which the poet John Clare called 'the March nightingale', singing from every patch of scrub. In the 1920s, Metroland brochures fêted real nightingales as one of the area's great attractions: 'The song of the nightingale for which the neighbourhood is renowned . . . the network of translucent rivers traversing the valley, render Rickmansworth a Mecca to the city man pining for country and pure air.' Nightingales were extinct here as breeding birds by the 1960s but are commemorated in one of the street names in the Cedars Estate. When I reach Stocker's and Springwell Lakes (two of the now flooded gravel pits) I see that they too have become a kind of commemoration of birds and are fully fledged nature reserves. Years back I saw my first red-crested pochard here, a winter vagrant from eastern Europe with a lurid crimson bill that made it the oddest, most plastic-looking wild duck I had ever seen, and rather appropriate bobbing on a man-made lake. What I didn't know then was that the links between the pits and Metroland were more than simply geographical. The sand excavated from the Colne valley beds was the raw material for the houses and avenues of the new estates. (One story from Wembley Park in the 1920s has a touch of black comedy. The building contract was originally with the disastrously named Cyclops Construction Company, which had difficulty getting labourers and raw materials out of London and went into liquidation. The Metropolitan Company itself took over the supply of sand from the Colne valley pits.)

I bypass Chorleywood and head towards my old retreats north of the line near Latimer, only this time I'm coming in from the south, via Chenies. Latimer is a bijou village, in which many Metro-edge rustic comedies and melodramas have been acted out. The exotic animals from Bertram Mills Circus were taken to winter quarters here, next to fields full of English dairy cows. On the Chesham shuttle line just to the west, a van loaded with hay from a nearby field tumbled down an embankment just in front of a homebound train. (The service was severely disrupted but no one was injured.) And by the side of the road I used to reluctantly follow home to Berkhamsted after my escapes to the Mediterranean ambience of the Chess valley, there is still a curious wooden board masking the spiked fence round a group of half-timbered cottages (authentic eighteenth century, not Metroland mimics). Lord Chesham ordered the board to be put up in the early 1920s, when his favourite dog died after being impaled on the fence. It's still there, a backhanded tribute to the power of the squirearchy that Metroland did so much to weaken.

But there is something hearteningly new here. Loitering in the trees by the edge of the Chess are a few little egrets, looking like starched shawls rather casually tossed into the fuzzy alder branches. Egrets began colonizing Britain in the 1990s and first reached the watery places of Metroland a decade later. They are a new generation of suburban settlers, immigrants from southern and eastern Europe, tempted north by global warming.

From here to the Met's current terminus at Amersham the landscape is pure Chilterns, the hanging beechwoods and sunken lanes and skewed pastures in which, for most of my adult life, I spent the time when I wasn't slumming in the edge-lands. Except that I'm increasingly aware, as I was back in Moor Park, of posters in cottage windows, nailed to trees, propped up in fields, all protesting at the imminent arrival of the High Speed Rail-Link, HS2, between London and the North. (Though only in the extreme western shires of Metroland could anyone get away with the poster I saw in one paddock: SCRAP HS2. SPEND THE MONEY ON THE ARMED FORCES.) I realize that, with the inexorable topographical logic of transport systems, its proposed route has been shadowing the Met all the way from the point it breaks out into open country, west of Northwood. HS2 will slam through the Harefield woods, loop just south of Chorleywood and Little Chalfont and thunder on towards Great Missenden. It's a folly, a commercially motivated enterprise whose real-world economic and environmental credentials have been well discredited. Yet oddly, it shares characteristics with both the Met and the M25. Like the Met, it trades in potential customers' dreams; and true to the spirit of the moment, these are now not of finding space but of saving time – about 20 minutes, it's reckoned, on the London to Birmingham leg, a journey which could be avoided altogether by businesspeople working on their iPads in the comfort of their Metro-pads. Like the M25, it promises a trip which is not a journey, with a real destination, but pure, ephemeral, disembodied travel.

Dear Amersham on the Hill, the end of the line, the settlement the Met conjured into existence half a mile above the old town, which the brochure of 1916 preposterously compared to 'the picturesque buildings of the times of

Shakespeare and Sir Christopher Wren'. It is the only place in Metroland where, in my thirties, I succumbed to the unalloyed suburban aura that so enchanted Betjeman. While he relished poignant late afternoons at the Chiltern Court restaurant above Baker Street station, I mooned about on winter's evenings 25 miles down the track in the real Chilterns, hanging out in Amersham's lamp-lit 1930s shopping centre, and bound for Ken's Beijing Chinese restaurant next to the railway bridge, an oriental eatery tucked inside what seemed like an old English cottage.

Early Electric! Sit you down and see,
  'Mid this fine woodwork and a smell of dinner,
A stained-glass windmill and a pot of tea,
  And sepia views of leafy lanes in PINNER, –
Then visualize, far down the shining lines,
  Your parents' homestead set in murmuring
  pines.

from 'The Metropolitan Railway',
John Betjeman

In the closing sequence of his film, Betjeman stands at the top of Amersham on the Hill, next to an architect-designed, 1930s *'moderne'* house called High and Over, and laments how the frumpier, late-phase Metroland development had ruined its lofty view towards the Chalfont woods. 'The end of high hopes and overambition,' he sighs, 'and perhaps the end of England too.' Then he is at the final frontier of the great project's ambition, leaning on a gate and gazing down a rough track that is all that remains of the extension from Verney Junction that might, had Sir Edward Watkin got his way, have headed off to the North through the immortalized Oxfordshire countryside of *Lark Rise to Candleford* five miles away. 'The houses of Metroland never got as far as Verney Junction. Grass triumphs, and I must say I am rather glad.'

Grass has triumphed, not just here, but all the way back down the track, and it is the proper answer to our national poet's pessimism about the end of England. By 'grass' Betjeman didn't mean the tidy lawns he'd witnessed being given their Sunday manicure in Pinner. He meant *turf*, the ground-base of pre-rail trackways, the obstinate growth that prospers the more you trample it, the slang for the patch you live in. 'Turf' teases the edges of Metroland from Chesham to Neasden. It's there in the sucking mud of the Welsh Harp, the ivy climbing the M25's support pillars, the terns' nest-islands in the Rickmansworth gravel pits, the feral line-side ash trees at Eastcote that still echo its 1920s 'farm-yard atmosphere'. And turf, in this sense, has given the citizens of Metroland a glimpse of the inventiveness and resilience of real nature.

The creation of Metroland did destroy swathes of ordinary farming countryside west of London. But it provided the chance, at least in its western reaches, for large numbers of people previously cooped up in dismal city terraces to experience a kind of sub-rural life. (Chorleywood West is reputed to have the highest indices of social satisfaction of any town in England.) The snobbish fun that was poked at them and their lifestyles (and still is, occasionally) might be more fairly aimed at the sentimental fantasies put out by the Metropolitan Railway's propaganda machine.

You could even say that they have the best of both kinds of green world: the tidy rose garden and the rampaging rosebay.

And now, out in the Amersham borderlands, they have been gifted with something rather magical and magnificent that even Selbie at his most profuse could not have predicted, and which, in a way, is a parable about the whole idea of Metroland. In the late 1980s the Nature Conservancy Council reintroduced the red kite, one of Europe's most charismatic birds of prey, to a patch of the Chilterns about twelve miles west of Amersham. The birds, fledglings brought over from colonies of wild birds in Spain, prospered. They went on to breed, and began to spread beyond their release site, west into Oxfordshire and north and east into the hill country on both sides of the Met Line.

Red kites were once common across Britain, in countryside and city alike. They're scavengers, and before the days of municipal sanitation, they played a crucial role in clearing meat debris and edible garbage from the streets.

Their sociability made them the beneficiaries of the UK's very first bird protection laws, back in the Middle Ages. But with the development of the keepered shooting estate in the late eighteenth century, they became rebranded as predatory vermin, and were shot, poisoned, gin-trapped and strangled, until by the end of the nineteenth century they were extinct in England.

The decision to reintroduce them was made for two reasons. The first was one of common justice, to bring home a once honoured and grossly abused British citizen. The second was more controversial. The red kite is captivatingly beautiful, especially in flight, and tolerant of human company, as it had been in the Middle Ages. It was thought that a reintroduction in the Chilterns, where, in true Metroland style, wild and inhabited land is intimately intertwined, might be good for humans and birds alike.

The gamble worked. The birds thrived. As their population built up, they became more conspicuous. They now float over the Met Line and the M25. They throng above town centres, and, at dusk, at their communal roosts in the woods. They've become the region's totems and transformed its attitude towards wildlife. Playgroups have been named after them. Traffic slows down when there are constellations overhead. And the well-heeled citizens of the Chilterns, far from quaking when these five-foot-wing-span, hooked-beak distillations of the wild venture into their gardens, have been putting whole chickens (and, it's mischievously rumoured, fillet steaks) on to their bird tables to tempt them in. A live kite in the garden beats a concrete statuette of Flora any day.

There have been grumbles from some conservationists about the damage such a convenience-food diet may be doing to the birds' constitutions (probably partly justified); and, more puritanically, that the affection of the public is in some way corrupting the kites' essential wildness, taming them, putting them in an invisible cage. But I've watched these birds closely for more than 20 years and I don't believe their wildness has been compromised one iota. A party wheeling over a likely garden at teatime may look a little like a gathering of opportunist street buskers, but you know that an hour later they will be about their imperious private business again. These are the notes I wrote one early spring in the Chilterns, after watching kites all day:

They could have been any birds in the distance, drifting in the grey sky. Then they lifted up, flexed, soared, two taut crossbows against the leafless ridge-woods. They glided towards me – no hurry, just riding the wind, sliding across the eddies. They came close, and I could see the rufous plumage ruffling on their bodies and tails. They were calling, but the wind carried their cries away from me. I drove further south, up on to the plateau. There were kites everywhere. They were sporting over the villages, lifting on gusts that took them sailing clean over cottages, then down to the level of the bird-tables. When I stopped for lunch in a pub I could see them through the windows, arcing across the hedges, huge and buoyant, using their forked tails as rudders. Outside I watched one close to as it turned into the wind. It raised its wings – as relaxed as a dancer's arms or a half-full jib-sail – and gathered the wind in, folded it into itself. It was so poised, so effortlessly muscular, that I could feel my own shoulders flexing in sympathy.

The red kite's mastery of flight is so total that I have seen a bird playing with a windblown feather, repeatedly flying up with it in its bill, then letting it fall and catching it close to the ground. And their easy intimacy with humans means that they regularly steal household bric-a-brac to line their nests – kids' toys, disposable plastic gloves, a pair of tights and, in the case of one particularly leery bird, several pairs of ladies' knickers grabbed from washing lines. And it's here that some ancient echoes begin to sound. Four hundred years ago, when red kites would have swarmed around east London and the Globe Theatre,

Shakespeare has Autolycus, the streetwise con man in *The Winter's Tale*, warn: 'When the kite builds, look to your lesser linen.'

Now the Chiltern kites are edging eastwards, back towards their old epicentre, along a route that roughly corresponds to that of the Metropolitan Line. They're seen regularly over Chorleywood and Moor Park golf course. They've been spotted high over Regent's Park, close to where Lord's station once stood. Doubtless they have passed over the 800-year-old Smithfield meat market – the medieval kite's choicest foraging ground – just a few hundred yards north of Farringdon, the original eastern terminus of the Met Line – as in January 2006, one arrived, pursued by a mob of crows and magpies, in a back garden in Hackney. The owner thought it was an eagle and called the police.

Unlike the citizens of Metroland, well used by now to cemetery foxes, feral grapevines on the embankments and tank traps from the Cretaceous era, Londoners are not quite ready for mighty birds of prey on their home turf. The original idea of Metroland was predicated on the essential difference between city and countryside. But what it showed instead was their seamless compatibility, their willingness to develop social and natural ecotones. And the kites are carrying the torch for this idea back into the heart of the city.

Further Reading

Julian Barnes, *Metroland* (London, Robin Clark, 1981)

John Betjeman, *Collected Poems*, 3rd edn (London, John Murray, 1970)

Clive Foxell, *The Metropolitan Line: London's First Underground Railway* (Stroud, The History Press, 2010)

Leslie Hepple, and Alison Doggett, *The Chilterns* (Chichester, Phillimore and Co., 1992)

Alan Jackson, *London's Metropolitan Railway* (Newton Abbot, David and Charles, 1986)

Alan Jackson, *London's Metro-land* (Harrow, Capital Transport, 2006)

Richard Mabey, *The Unofficial Countryside* (London, Collins, 1973)

Richard Mabey, *Home Country* (London, Century, 1990)

Richard Mabey, *Nature Cure* (London, Chatto & Windus, 2005)

Andrew Martin, *Underground, Overground: A Passenger's History of the Tube* (London, Profile, 2012)

George Orwell, *The Collected Essays, Journalism and Letters* (London, Secker & Warburg, 1968)

Iain Sinclair, *London Orbital* (London, Granta, 2002)

Tiresias, *Notes from Overground: Man is Born Free, and is Everywhere in Trains* (London, Paladin, 1984)

The TV documentary *Metro-land*, written and narrated by John Betjeman and directed by Edward Mirzoeff, was first broadcast on BBC One on 26 February 1973.

PENGUIN LINES

Choose Your Journey

If you're looking for...

Romantic Encounters

Heads and Straights
by Lucy Wadham
(the Circle line)

Waterloo–City, City–Waterloo
by Leanne Shapton
(the Waterloo & City line)

Tales of Growing Up and Moving On

Heads and Straights
by Lucy Wadham
(the Circle line)

A Good Parcel of English Soil
by Richard Mabey
(the Metropolitan line)

Mind the Child
by Camila Batmanghelidjh and
Kids Company
(the Victoria line)

The 32 Stops
by Danny Dorling
(the Central line)

*A History of Capitalism
According to the Jubilee Line*
by John O'Farrell
(the Jubilee line)

A Northern Line Minute
by William Leith
(the Northern line)

Mind the Child
by Camila Batmanghelidjh and
Kids Company
(the Victoria line)

Heads and Straights
by Lucy Wadham
(the Circle line)

**Laughter and
Tears**

**Breaking
Boundaries**

Drift
by Philippe Parreno
(the Hammersmith & City line)

Buttoned-Up
by Fantastic Man
(the East London line)

Waterloo–City, City–Waterloo
by Leanne Shapton
(the Waterloo & City line)

Earthbound
by Paul Morley
(the Bakerloo line)

Mind the Child
by Camila Batmanghelidjh
and Kids Company
(the Victoria line)

The Blue Riband
by Peter York
(the Piccadilly line)

**A Bit of
Politics**

The 32 Stops
by Danny Dorling
(the Central line)

*A History of Capitalism
According to the Jubilee Line*
by John O'Farrell
(the Jubilee line)

**Musical
Direction**

Heads and Straights
by Lucy Wadham
(the Circle line)

Earthbound
by Paul Morley
(the Bakerloo line)

The Blue Riband
by Peter York
(the Piccadilly line)

Tube Knowledge

What We Talk About When We Talk About The Tube
by John Lanchester
(the District line)

A Good Parcel of English Soil
by Richard Mabey
(the Metropolitan line)

A Breath of Fresh Air

A Good Parcel of English Soil
by Richard Mabey
(the Metropolitan line)

Design for Life

Waterloo–City, City–Waterloo
by Leanne Shapton
(the Waterloo & City line)

Buttoned-Up
by Fantastic Man
(the East London line)

Drift
by Philippe Parreno
(the Hammersmith & City line)